CHINA
the culture

Bobbie Kalman

A Bobbie Kalman Book

The Lands, Peoples, and Cultures Series

Crabtree Publishing Company
www.crabtreebooks.com

The Lands, Peoples, and Cultures Series

Created by Bobbie Kalman

For my aunt Margaret

Written by
Bobbie Kalman

Coordinating editor
Ellen Rodger

Editor
Jane Lewis

Contributing editor
Lisa Gurusinghe

Editors/first edition
Janine Schaub
Christine Arthurs
Margaret Hoogeveen

Production coordinator
Rose Gowsell

Production
Arlene Arch

Separations and film
Embassy Graphics

Printer
Worzalla Publishing Company

Illustrations
Halina Below-Spada: p. 6, 18, 30
Dianne Eastman: icons
Tina Holdcroft: p. 24-25
David Wysotski, Allure Illustrations: back cover

Photographs
Jim Bryant: p. 10 (both), 11; courtesy of the Consulate General of the People's Republic of China: p. 22; Dennis Cox/ChinaStock: p. 1, 5 (top left & right), 7 (top two), 8 (bottom right), 12 (top right, left, bottom), 13, 16, 17 (top), 21 (inset), 26, 28 (bottom); David Butz p. 27 (bottom); Ken Ginn: p. 31; Wolfgang Kaehler: p. 7 (bottom two), 15 (left), 17 (inset), 29 (bottom); Christopher Liu/ChinaStock: p. 4, 15 (right), 23, 27 (top), 28 (top), 29 (top), 30; Ivanka Lupenic: 14 (left); Gayle McDougall: p. 8 (top); Pat Morrow/First Light: p. 21 (top); courtesy of the Royal Ontario Museum: p. 9; Ron Schroeder: p. 5 (bottom); Caroline Walker: p. 8 (bottom left), 14 (right); Liu Xiaoyang/China Stock: p. 20; other images by Digital Stock

Every effort has been made to obtain the appropriate credit and full copyright clearance for all images in this book. Any oversights or omissions will be corrected in future editions.

Cover: A Peking Opera performer in dramatic makeup backstage at Beijing's Chang 'an Theater

Title page: An early morning outdoor tai chi class.

Back cover: The Giant Panda lives in the bamboo forests and mountain regions of southwestern China.

Published by
Crabtree Publishing Company

PMB 16A
350 Fifth Avenue
Suite 3308
New York
N.Y. 10118

612 Welland Avenue
St. Catharines
Ontario, Canada
L2M 5V6

73 Lime Walk
Headington
Oxford OX3 7AD
United Kingdom

Cataloging in Publication Data
Kalman, Bobbie
    China, the culture / Bobbie Kalman. – Rev. ed.
    p.cm – (The lands, peoples, and cultures series)
    Includes index.
    ISBN 0-7787-9380-X (RLB) – ISBN 0-7787-9748-1 (pbk.)
        1. China–Social life and customs–Juvenile literature.
2. China–Civilization–Juvenile literature. [1. China–Civilization.]
I. Title. II Series.
    DS721 .K1713 2001
    951–dc21   00-057079
                                                                        LC

Contents

A new pride in culture

The people of China have experienced a tremendous period of change in the last one hundred years. During this period of political turmoil they had little time or energy for cultural activities. Sometimes people were fighting in wars to save their country. In the mid-1900s the government in power discouraged or even outlawed activities such as painting, dancing, playing music, and religious worship. People were punished for having an interest in arts that did not have government approval. This period of cultural oppression was known as the Cultural Revolution.

In the last few decades China's **culture** has experienced a revival. People are rediscovering their **traditions**. They are once again celebrating traditional festivals and practicing their chosen religions. Painters, musicians, and writers all over the country are busy creating new works. The people of China are experiencing a renewed love for their arts and a new pride in their culture.

(opposite, top left) The Tibetan people are trying to maintain their own unique culture within China.

(below) These colorfully dressed citizens are celebrating the Chinese New Year.

(above) In a workshop in Beijing, vases are painted in traditional Chinese style.

(below) These young women from the Yunnan province are showing off their traditional costumes.

Ingenious inventions

In the ancient past China's culture was more advanced than that of any other country. In those days Europeans had never seen creations such as the ones invented by the Chinese. Adventurers and merchants sailed to China to bring these treasured objects back to their countries. The clock, printing press, compass, wheelbarrow, crossbow, and animal harness, as well as **porcelain**, ink, and playing cards are just a few of the inventions the Chinese have passed on to the rest of the world.

Flying high

Perhaps you love to fly a kite on windy days. The Chinese were the first people ever to fly kites. They are still such avid kite fans that a Kite Festival is held every year in April. On this day everyone climbs a hill or finds an open area for flying kites and having fun.

The Chinese are experts at making kites. They make colorful kites in the shapes of dragons, birds, butterflies, and centipedes. Some animal-shaped kites are designed so they can roll their eyes and flutter their wings. Other kites are so big that they require four or five people to operate them!

Mulberry bark paper

In ancient China written records were kept on strips of bamboo that were tied together. These documents were difficult to store because they took up too much room. In A.D. 105 Ts'ai Lun, an official with the imperial court, had an ingenious idea. He made a mushy mixture of mulberry bark, **hemp**, rags, water, and old fish nets. He pressed the pulp into a thin sheet and allowed it to dry. The result was the first piece of paper!

Exploding bamboo

The first fireworks were made by stuffing gunpowder into hollow sticks of bamboo. Gunpowder is thought to have been discovered by accident—by medicine men who were trying to invent new cures for illness. The Chinese people adopted the use of gunpowder as a way to scare off evil spirits and ghosts. The tradition of lighting fireworks on holidays is still popular in China today. The loud bangs and pops of fireworks are believed to ensure good luck by scaring off bad spirits.

The compass

The Chinese were the first to discover that a magnetic object could indicate direction by pointing in a north-south direction. In ancient times, the Chinese used a **lodestone** to locate suitable burial sites. In later days, travelers used it to guide them in the right direction. The lodestone was eventually replaced by a magnetized needle in a device called a compass.

The abacus

In China, students and business people use the abacus for making calculations. An abacus is a hand-operated device that consists of rows of beads on metal rods set in a rectangular wooden frame. The Chinese invented this counting instrument in the second century B.C. Some Chinese are so skilled that they can solve a mathematical problem on an abacus faster than someone using an electronic calculator!

Guarding the secret of silk

In earlier days, European traders traveled all the way to China to buy a fine, smooth fabric called silk. For many years, the Chinese kept the secret of silk production to themselves. They knew that silk was made from the cocoons of tiny silkworms. **Western** people eventually learned the secret of silk-making, but the Chinese are still famous for the quality and beauty of their silk fabrics.

How silk is made

Producing silk is a lengthy process. It takes 40,000 silkworms to produce just twelve pounds (5.5 kg) of silk! The pictures on this page show the steps of silk-making. Match the information below to the pictures.

• After silkworm eggs are hatched in a warm room, baby worms feed on mulberry leaves until they are very fat. Thousands of feeding worms are kept on trays that are stacked one on top of another. A roomful of munching worms sounds like heavy rain falling on a roof.

• The silkworms feed until they have stored up enough energy to enter the cocoon stage. When it is time to build their cocoons, the worms produce a jelly-like substance in their silk glands, which hardens when it comes into contact with air. Silkworms use this substance to spin a cocoon around themselves until they look like puffy, white balls. It takes three or four days to spin a cocoon.

• After eight or nine days in a warm, dry place the cocoons are ready to be unwound. First they are steamed or baked to kill the **pupas**, or worms. The cocoons are dipped into hot water to loosen the tightly woven strands. Then the strands are unwound onto a spool. Each cocoon is made up of a thread between 1968 and 2,953 feet (600 and 900 m) long! Between five and eight of these super-fine strands are twisted together to make one silk thread.

• Finally the silk threads are woven into cloth or used for embroidery work. Clothes made from silk are not only beautiful and lightweight, they are also warm in cool weather and cool in hot weather!

Traditional arts

The Chinese are famous for their traditional arts. Painting and calligraphy, **sculpture**, architecture, and the creation of fine porcelain are just a few of the arts that date far back into the history of Chinese culture.

(above) The scene pictured is part of a painted ceiling at the Summer Palace near Beijing.

Calligraphy

The art of fine writing is called calligraphy. The first great Chinese calligraphers lived 1,600 years ago. In ancient times, the Chinese people thought calligraphy to be the most beautiful art form. Artists were highly respected because it took great skill to master the difficult brushstrokes.

Delicate brushstrokes

Calligraphy is still important in modern China. When children learn to read and write, they also learn calligraphy's delicate brushstrokes. The thousands of complicated **pictographs** that make up the Chinese alphabet are based on the eight brushstrokes of calligraphy. The basic tools for calligraphy are called the four treasures of the study. They are paper, ink, ink stone, and brush.

Calligraphers often write out poems in fine script using black ink and brushes made from animal hair. Chinese writing is well suited to poetry because many of its pictographs resemble the idea they are communicating. For example, the character for "way" or "path" looks something like a foot striding forward, as if a person were actually walking down a path.

Painting

Traditional Chinese painting is based on the eight brushstrokes that are used in calligraphy. Many other brushstrokes are used as well, each with a certain purpose. For example, a particular stroke is used for painting bamboo, another for trees, and one for rocks and mountains. Many Chinese paintings depict nature. Landscapes and symbolic birds and flowers are popular subjects.

These works of art are painted on long panels of paper or silk. Fans, screens, and wall and ceiling panels are also painted. A painted handscroll made of silk or paper is read by slowly unrolling the scroll for viewers to see. A poem often accompanies the painting to help people understand the meaning of the picture.

Precious porcelain

Pottery was one of the first crafts of ancient China. The finest of all pottery is porcelain, which the Chinese invented in the ninth century. Porcelain is made from a mixture of coal dust and a fine, white clay called kaolin. Ordinary ceramics are fired, or baked, at around 932°F (500°C). Porcelain is fired at temperatures of more than 2100°F (1150°C). It is then glazed and fired again to make it shiny. This process makes the porcelain hard, thin, and translucent.

Plain yet beautiful

Porcelain is naturally white or cream colored. The early pieces were left in this original state. Artists began using dyes in the thirteenth century. A deep blue dye made from a mineral called cobalt was especially popular. This dye was used to create the beautiful blue-and-white vases made during the Ming dynasty, which have become famous all over the world.

China's china

A few centuries ago Chinese porcelain was in such great demand that merchants from many countries sailed to China to trade for it. It soon became known as china. Today people use this term, not only for porcelain, but for all kinds of dishes and pottery. Although most porcelain is now made in factories, much of it is still painted by hand.

(left) A beautiful Ming vase.

(opposite left) The calligraphy of Confucius, Mao Zedong, and others are displayed on brass plates in museums.

(opposite right) A young girl practices the art of calligraphy.

9

Living rock

In ancient China, the ability to sculpt was considered a skill rather than an art. Great sculptures were created to express religious devotion. Images of **Buddha** carved out of natural rock formations are among China's most spectacular works of art. Some of these carvings are as tall as five-story buildings. They are so lifelike that they certainly deserve the nickname "living rock!"

Thousands of Buddhas

In clusters of caves in northern China, thousands of images of Buddha have been carved into the cave walls. The oldest of these are the Dunhuang Caves in which dedicated monks carved Buddhas and painted the walls for over ten centuries. There are 492 caves containing more than 2,000 sculptures of the Buddha and some 59,800 square yards (50,000 m²) of beautiful religious wall paintings. The Yungang Grottoes near Datong contain the largest and most beautiful cave sculptures in China. Although many caves have been deteriorating, fifty-three of them survive, containing over 50,000 images of the Buddha, angels, and animals. Some are over fifty-six feet (17 m) high.

Traditional architecture

Although Chinese civilization is thousands of years old, only a few ancient buildings are still standing. Most of China's early buildings were made of wood, which has decayed over time. Wood was used to build homes and temples because the Chinese liked its natural qualities. The oldest building in China is a wooden temple built in the year 782.

Colorful buildings with curved, upswept eaves, bright roof tiles, and carved adornments are all part of traditional Chinese architecture. The dragon, crane, phoenix, unicorn, and other **symbols** are painted or carved into the walls and roof supports. These animals symbolize good fortune and long life.

The way buildings are constructed and decorated has meaning in Chinese culture. Red is used to bring good fortune, and yellow is the emperor's color. The number of steps or columns usually represents important things such as the four seasons of the year or the five virtues of Buddhism. Nine is the emperor's number.

The Chinese use a set of principles called *feng shui* to determine how their buildings can be in harmony with the surrounding environment to bring them good fortune. For example, buildings face south because north is thought to be the source of evil. Chinese buildings are often planned with the help of *feng shui* masters whose job it is to ensure that buildings will bring the best fortune to their future residents.

Pretty pagodas

Perhaps the most striking example of architecture in China is the pagoda, even though the design originally came from India. Pagodas look like several one-story buildings stacked on top of one another, with each story having its own roof. Some pagodas are square; others have many sides. Some are made of wood; others are of stone. The highest ones are the most sacred. Pagodas can be found at Buddhist temples and contain religious **relics**. They are not designed as dwellings. In fact, they usually have solid cores!

(top and bottom) Chinese opera singers wear elaborate costumes and makeup.

Amazing circus acrobats

Imagine trying to balance another person on your head while standing on top of a stack of ten chairs! Acrobats must be very agile and flexible to perform stunts such as spinning plates on tall poles or juggling while walking on a giant ball. For 2,000 years professional Chinese acrobats have been performing these difficult and spectacular tricks. Today acrobatic and circus troupes continue to amaze audiences throughout China and around the world.

A night at the opera

The opera is a popular form of entertainment in China. Operas are at least three hours long. At one time they lasted up to three days! Although the songs in a Chinese opera may be hard to understand, even for someone who speaks Chinese, the viewer can still understand what is going on from the gestures, makeup, and costumes. A trembling body, for example, means fear, and crossed eyes show anger. The villain always has a white patch on his nose.

There are many different styles of opera, each one originating from a different region. Of all the styles, the most famous is the Beijing Opera. It features high-pitched singing, elaborate costumes, and a large **percussion** section. Beijing operas are often based on historical events.

Shadow puppets

Shadow-puppet shows are sometimes called the "opera of the common man." The stories are the same as those of the grand operas, but they are presented with only a few props. Puppeteers move their puppets between a bright light and a screen or sheet to create a shadow effect.

(right) After school, these children learn how to play the pipa.

(opposite, top right) There are about eighty acrobatic troupes in China that perform breathtaking balancing acts.

Chinese music

When the Cultural Revolution came to an end, the Chinese government started encouraging people to take up cultural activities such as music once again. Although western music is popular in China now, the Chinese also have great pride in their traditional music. The Conservatory of Chinese Music and other schools have begun training musicians in this art. People all over China are attending concerts in which typical Chinese instruments, such as the *hu qin*, the *pipa* lute, and *sheng* pipes, are played.

The main instrument in the Chinese orchestra is the *hu qin*. It has two strings and is played with a bow. The *pipa* lute has more strings and is plucked like a guitar. Many children are learning to play the pipa. Chinese flutes, such as the *xiao*, are made of bamboo. The most traditional Chinese instrument is the *sheng* pipe, which is made of several bamboo reeds.

Chinese cuisine

Chinese cooking is known for its variety of flavors and textures and by its many different cooking styles. Steaming and stir-frying are the most common ways to cook food in China. Besides these, there are over eighty other cooking techniques. In China chefs are so highly regarded for their cooking skills that they are sometimes called "doctors of food."

Fresh and fast

Chinese food is prepared with the freshest ingredients. Bite-sized pieces cook quickly and can be eaten easily with chopsticks. Stir-frying food in a wok is one of the most popular cooking methods. Only a small amount of oil is needed in this deep, round frying pan. Stir-frying food in hot oil preserves the nutritional value of the food. Great attention is paid to the colors and presentation of the food.

Chinese cooks do not like to waste anything. Whether from land or sea, almost every type and part of an animal is eaten, including eels, sea slugs, snakes, jellyfish, chicken feet, and duck tongues. Imaginative names are also characteristic of Chinese cuisine. Eight-jewel Duck, Red-cooked Lion's Head, and Gold Coin are just a few examples of Chinese dishes.

Regional cooking styles

There are five major styles of Chinese cooking: Canton, Fukien, Honan, Sichuan, and Shantung. The Cantonese style originates from the region around Guangzhou (once known as Canton) and is the most familiar to Westerners. Dishes such as egg rolls, chop suey, and chow mein are all part of Cantonese cooking. A mild climate and access to the sea give the chefs of this area a wide variety of ingredients from which to choose. Cantonese cooks follow the Daoist principle that food should be eaten as near to its natural state as possible. It should be fresh and cooked only for a short time.

Fukien, Honan, and Sichuan

The province of Fukien has a long sea coast, so a wide variety of seafood is available to its residents. Fukien cuisine is well known for its delicate flavors and clear soups. Cooks of Honan were the first to produce the famous Chinese sweet-and-sour sauce and the deep-fried method of cooking. Sichuan cooking is famous for spicy foods that can set your mouth on fire! Sichuan dishes are made with red-chili and peppercorn pastes, fermented rice, and brown sugar. The result is hot, sweet, and sour flavors.

A wok is used to prepare many Chinese dishes.

Eels are just one of many foods sold at the market.

(below) This man holds his bowl of rice close to his mouth to use chopsticks.

(above) This family is sharing a Mongolian hot pot meal.

Shantung

The Shantung style of cooking comes from the north. It is best known for duck soup and Peking Duck. Peking Duck is a delicacy that comes from Beijing, which used to be known as Peking. The waiter announces the arrival of this fabulous dish at the table by striking a gong. Flavorings such as soya sauce, garlic, and black and red bean pastes are also popular. Little rice is farmed in the north, so wheat noodles and dumplings serve as the northern residents' staple starchy foods. They also enjoy lamb dishes.

The Mongolian Hot Pot

The Mongolian Hot Pot came to China during the time the **Mongols** ruled the country. It is a famous northern fondue-style meal that is centered around a pot filled with boiling soup stock. A variety of raw meat is arranged in dishes around the pot. The diners cook their own meals by dipping pieces of meat into the boiling broth. The meat cooks quickly and adds flavor to the boiling stock. Several sauces, such as hot mustard, peanut, and soya, go with the meat. After the diners have finished their meat, they drink the flavorful broth to which vegetables such as spinach and cabbage have been added.

Eating Chinese style

The traditional Chinese table is round to allow guests to be at an equal distance from the food. Each place setting has bowls, a spoon, sauces, and chopsticks. Dishes are brought in one at a time, and the diners serve themselves from a platter. When eating with chopsticks, you should remember two things: never to touch your mouth with the chopsticks and never cross your chopsticks when you have finished your meal. Both of these actions are considered bad manners. To learn how to use chopsticks, see page 30.

All the tea in China

No Chinese meal is complete without a pot of hot tea. In fact, the Chinese introduced the rest of the world to this popular beverage. Tea is still an important part of Chinese culture. It is sipped at every meal, offered to all guests, and served in local teahouses. It is believed to have a calming effect, and some herbal teas serve medicinal purposes. The Chinese prepare tea by pouring boiling water over loose tea leaves. The flavorful brew is drunk without milk or sugar from small cups without handles. Chinese teas come in all kinds of colors and flavors, such as green, yellow, red, mint, and flower-blossom.

 # Old and new beliefs

Chinese folk religion is filled with gods, demons, and spirits. Many of China's traditional festivals are based on ancient **myths** about these supernatural creatures. Old practices, such as offering gifts to the gods, are part of Chinese folk religion. The Chinese also worship their **ancestors**, who are believed to possess the power to help or hinder their living descendants.

Yin and *Yang*

Many Chinese believe that the universe is made up of two forces: *yin* and *yang*. *Yin* is feminine and *yang* is masculine. *Yin* and *yang* are opposites that work together to create a balance. Examples of *yin* are characteristics such as soft, right, and cold. These are balanced out by the *yang* qualities of hard, left, and warm. The well-being of the world, the body, and the soul are believed to depend on these forces staying in balance.

The teachings of Confucius

Confucius introduced a set of moral ethics by which many Chinese people lived. Confucius was a scholar who lived from 551 to 479 B.C.

According to Confucius, the ideal person was polite, honest, courageous, and wise. For more than 2,000 years Chinese society was based on the Confucian code of behavior. Children were taught to obey their parents, and everyone was expected to respect the elderly and obey the rulers of the country.

Laotzu and Taoism

Taoism is also very old. It is based on a short book called the *Tao te Ching*, written by a man known as Laotzu, who lived around the same time as Confucius. Taoists believe that achieving the balance of the *yin* and *yang* is the key to achieving spiritual peace. Taoism teaches the importance of harmony with nature and encourages a simple way of life. Both Confucianism and Taoism have deeply affected the characters of the Chinese people over the centuries.

The yin *and* yang *contain the seeds of each other.*

(top) Monks participate in a ceremony at the Jade Buddha Temple in Shanghai.

Buddhism

Centuries ago, a man named Sakyamuni lived in India. One day while meditating, he discovered the meaning of life and how to end the suffering of all people. He became the Buddha, which means the "Awakened One." Those who follow his teachings believe that people are born over and over again as human beings, animals, or insects. If you do good deeds in this life, your next life will be a good one. But if you live a life of evil, your next life will be full of misfortune.

Buddhism came to China from India in the fifth century B.C. Over the years China has developed its own version called Chan Buddhism, also known as Zen Buddhism, a mix of Taoist and Buddhist beliefs. Tibetans and Mongols practice a version of Buddhism called Lama Buddhism.

(top) These taoist monks are reciting prayers in the White Cloud Temple in Baiyunguan.

(inset) A golden Buddha statue sits at the front of a temple.

Islam and Christianity

In China there are fewer Muslims and Christians than Buddhists. Islam was founded at Mecca, Saudi Arabia, by a **prophet** named Muhammed. It was brought to China by Arab traders in the seventh century. The Kazaks and Uygurs who live in the western regions follow the Islamic faith. Christianity, which is based on the teachings of Jesus Christ, was introduced to China in the sixteenth century by European **missionaries**.

New freedom

When China became a **communist** country in 1949, the Chinese were not allowed to practice any religion. Many religious buildings were destroyed. In 1982, the Chinese government declared that all citizens were once again allowed religious freedom. Many temples, monasteries, and churches are being restored or rebuilt. Some people argue, however, that the Chinese people still do not have true religious freedom.

Chinese symbols

Over the centuries the Chinese have created many symbols to express the values that are important to them. Signs, colors, and even animals symbolize such things as long life, happiness, peace, and beauty.

Shou — The *shou* sign was adapted from the Chinese character or pictograph that means long life. It appears everywhere—sewn onto silk, carved in jade, and painted on porcelain.

Fu — The sign for happiness also comes from the Chinese language. The character *fu* is often surrounded by bats because fu also means bat.

Dragon — The dragon is a symbol representing the country of China, rain, and spring. According to an ancient Chinese legend, the dragon was the god of rain. Clouds formed when he breathed. In spring he brought the rain; in winter he buried himself in the mud at the bottom of the sea. He is a symbol of spring and new life.

Phoenix — The phoenix is an imaginary bird that looks something like a peacock. It is a symbol of beauty, peace, the summer harvest, and long life. When pictured together, the dragon and phoenix foretell good luck, so they are often used as wedding decorations.

Unicorn — The Chinese unicorn looks different from the ones you may have seen in pictures. The unicorn is a Buddhist symbol of wisdom, so it is sometimes shown carrying a law book.

Tortoise — The tortoise is a symbol of the universe. Its round back represents the sky, and its belly the earth. The tortoise is a symbol of strength and long life because it was believed to live for a thousand years.

Lion — Sculptures of lions are often placed as guards outside important buildings. A male lion is usually shown playing with a ball. A female lion has a tiny cub under her paw.

shou, *the sign of long life*

fu, *the sign of happiness*

18

Astrology is the study of how the stars and planets are related to a person's fortune and well-being. In western astrology, a person's fortune is predicted by observing the location of the stars and planets on the day of his or her birth. The ancient Chinese horoscope predicts that people born in a certain year have a particular set of characteristics.

Animal characteristics

A Chinese legend tells the story of a time when all the animals of the world were invited to come and visit the Buddha. Only twelve animals came. In order to reward these animals for their loyalty, the Buddha named a year after each one in the order they appeared before him. The cycle of animal names repeats every twelve years. The people born in the year of a certain animal are believed to have some of the characteristics of that animal. For instance, if you were born in 1992, the year of the monkey, you may be clever and impatient, just as a monkey is thought to be! Look at the following chart to see what traits you and your friends have. What other characteristics describe your personality?

Your year	Are these your traits?
Year of the Rat 1960, 1972, 1984, 1996, 2008	• You are charming, fussy, and a penny pincher. Only through love will you become generous.
Year of the Ox 1961, 1973, 1985, 1997, 2009	• You are quiet and patient until angered. You inspire confidence. You are also stubborn.
Year of the Tiger 1962, 1974, 1986, 1998, 2010	• You are courageous. Sometimes you are selfish. Though sympathetic, you can be suspicious.
Year of the Rabbit 1963, 1975, 1987, 1999, 2011	• You are fortunate and well-respected. Sometimes you are a daydreamer.
Year of the Dragon 1964, 1976, 1988, 2000, 2012	• You are healthy, energetic, short-tempered, and stubborn. You are honest and brave.
Year of the Snake 1965, 1977, 1989, 2001, 2013	• You are quiet and wise and like to dress up. You help other people but tend to overdo it.
Year of the Horse 1954, 1966, 1978, 1990, 2002	• You are independent. You talk too much. You are popular but sometimes you trust the wrong people.
Year of the Sheep 1955, 1967, 1979, 1991, 2003	• You are gentle in your ways. Sometimes you are pessimistic. You are a very cultured person.
Year of the Monkey 1956, 1968, 1980, 1992, 2004	• You are a genius, but you are not steady. Though clever and skillful, you can be impatient.
Year of the Rooster 1957, 1969, 1981, 1993, 2005	• Only sometimes are you fortunate. You work hard, but you often take on too much.
Year of the Dog 1958, 1970, 1982, 1994, 2006	• You have a deep sense of loyalty and duty. Your tongue is sharp, but you keep secrets well.
Year of the Boar 1959, 1971, 1983, 1995, 2007	• You are brave and can do anything you decide to do. You have few friends, but they last for life.

Colorful and noisy parades

In China many festivals are connected with national celebrations. Labor Day, Women's Day, Children's Day, and Army Day are just a few of these. The most important celebrations in modern China are Liberation Day and Chinese New Year.

National Day

On October 1, 1949, **Mao Zedong** announced the founding of the People's Republic of China. National Day is now celebrated every year on October 1. It is the biggest national holiday in China. People from all over the country gather in Beijing to take part in a huge parade on Qang Street. They wave banners and march past the Gate of Heavenly Peace. After the parade, thousands go to the park in the Forbidden City for fireworks, singing, and dancing.

The Lunar Calendar

Chinese people use the **lunar** calendar to count the passing of years. This ancient calendar is based on the cycles of the moon. A month starts when the new moon appears in the sky. According to the lunar calendar, one year has thirteen months.

Spring Festival

Chinese New Year, also known as the Spring Festival, falls in early spring. The Chinese New Year is held on the first day of the first lunar month, which occurs at the end of January or beginning of February. The celebrations last for an entire week.

An ancient Chinese legend says that a long time ago, there was a monster who ate people. The gods decided to lock him up inside a mountain to protect the population from being devoured. Once a year, however, during New Year, the gods allowed him to come out. The Chinese kept him away from their homes by lighting firecrackers. The monster was frightened away by the flashing and banging. This bright, noisy display has become a tradition at midnight every New Year.

(below) The dragon dance helps ring in the Chinese New Year.

(opposite, top) Liberation Day is celebrated with colorful parades.

Making preparations

Spring Festival is a big celebration, and everyone prepares for the event well in advance. People begin by setting up an altar for Zao Wang, the lord of the stove. At one time a picture of Zao Wang hung by the kitchen stove in every home. People believed that he went up to heaven during the Spring Festival and reported to the gods about each household. If the report was good, the gods would look after the family throughout the rest of the year. To make sure Zao Wang had sweet things to say, the Chinese spread honey on his mouth! Before the New Year arrives, people try to pay back debts and rid their hearts of grudges towards others.

A family time

During Spring Festival, families visit the tombs of their dead relatives. They honor their ancestors by lighting **incense** and burning imitation money. Afterwards, they go back to their homes for a huge feast. Children are given little red packets filled with money, and their parents let them stay up late.

(inset) These children in Inner Mongolia wear bright clothes to celebrate the Naadam festival.

Dancing dragons

On the third day of the Spring Festival there is a parade of dragon and lion dancers. The dragon costume has a papier-mâché head and a long, colorful, sequin-covered body. The dragon is so huge, it takes two people to hold up its head and twelve more to act as its legs. The streets are crowded and the sound of firecrackers can be heard throughout the parade. As the dragon passes everyone's home, people open their doors to let in the good luck that the dragon brings. Some people write rhymes in their best calligraphy and hang them on their doorways.

In China, people celebrate festivals that date back to ancient times. Although many traditional festivals were replaced by national festivals at the beginning of the Cultural Revolution, people in **rural** areas often continued to celebrate in the old ways. Most traditional festivals correspond to important dates on the old Chinese calendar.

There are fifty-six **national groups** in China, all with their own cultures and celebrations. Some of these groups take part in the traditional Chinese festivals, adding their own customs to the celebrations. They dress in traditional costumes, play instruments, or perform local folk dances.

Harvest Moon Festival

Food is important to everyone, so celebrating the harvest is one of the most important holidays around the world. It is no different in China. The Chinese celebrate this special time of thanksgiving with the Harvest Moon Festival.

On the evening of the Harvest Moon Festival, people climb hills and mountains to get a good view of the full moon. They carry fish- and bird-shaped paper lanterns. They give thanks for the harvest to the bright full moon of the eighth lunar month. Sometimes people also burn moon papers. Moon papers have pictures of rabbits and toads on them. According to Chinese mythology, a rabbit and a three-legged toad live on the moon. They are the moon's companions.

Sweet moon cakes

On the eve of the festival, friends and relatives give each other mouthwatering pastries called moon cakes. These small cakes contain a variety of sweet fillings, such as almond paste, red bean paste, or eggs. They are baked in molds, and an egg-yolk glaze gives them a shiny look. They often have flower or leaf designs on top. Moon cakes are always piled thirteen high—one cake for every month of the Chinese calendar.

An old legend recounts how moon cakes once saved the Chinese. A long time ago, China was ruled by people from foreign countries. The Chinese wanted the foreigners to leave the country. At the Harvest Moon Festival they hid messages inside moon cakes and passed them around to let everyone know of a secret plan to gain back control of China. At the arranged time, they gathered together and succeeded in overthrowing their cruel rulers.

(left) The Miao are one of China's minority groups. This Miao musician celebrates a festival wearing a fancy feather headdress. He accompanies traditional Miao folk dancers with a tune played on a type of sheng pipe.

Harvest moon cookies

Harvest moon cakes are difficult to make, but you can make our version of harvest moon cookies instead! Here are the ingredients you will need for the cookie dough:

1 cup (250 mL) softened butter
1/2 cup (125 mL) icing sugar
2 tsp (10 mL) vanilla
1 cup (250 mL) ground blanched almonds
1 1/2 cups (375 mL) sifted all-purpose flour

Cream butter with a big spoon. Sift sugar and gradually mix with the butter. Blend in vanilla and almonds, and slowly knead in flour. Put dough into refrigerator for one hour.

The fun part

Once the dough is chilled, it is ready for rolling. Sprinkle some flour on your rolling pin and on the kitchen counter. Roll out your dough to a thickness of 1/3 of an inch (1 cm). Now you can cut or form it into shapes! An upside-down glass works well as a full-moon-shaped cookie cutter. Make a crescent-shaped moon by cutting a full moon into two halves and pulling at the two ends until it looks like a crescent shape. To make a rabbit or a toad, cut the shapes out on a piece of paper, press the paper down on the rolled-out dough, and trim around the shape. Bake the cookies on a greased cookie sheet in a preheated 350°F (180°C) oven for fifteen minutes.

(above) During the Harvest Moon Festival, family and friends gather together to celebrate the harvest. They eat many delicious treats, including traditional pastries called Harvest Moon cakes.

The Lantern Festival

The Lantern Festival comes two weeks after the Spring Festival. During this celebration people carry candlelit lanterns shaped like goldfish, birds, and red globes. Rows of lanterns floating in the darkness is a beautiful sight. Sometimes groups of children perform a lantern dance.

Qing Ming Festival

The Qing Ming Festival takes place in April. It is a time when Chinese people honor the dead. People tend the graves of deceased relatives with great care. They pull weeds, plant flowers, and sweep around the grave sites. The family then shares a picnic lunch and burns sticks of incense in honor of their ancestors. Over the years, the festival has also come to honor those who fought and died in the revolutionary war.

Festival of Ice and Snow

In the northern Chinese city of Harbin, winter temperatures can fall below -22°F (-30°C). The citizens of this city have a yearly festival which helps them enjoy the cold weather. They construct huge ice sculptures in the shapes of animals, plants, and buildings. Some have names such as Moon Palace and Vivid Pagoda. They make ice lanterns by hollowing out a block of ice and putting a colored light inside. They are used to light up the sculptures at night.

The Dragon Boat Festival

The Dragon Boat Festival is celebrated in southern China. It is held in rememberance of the politician and poet Qu Yuan. In 288 B.C. Qu Yuan ended his life by throwing himself into the Miluo River in Hunan Province to protest the corrupt government. People respected Qu Yuan and wanted to find him and give him a proper funeral and burial. They launched their boats and threw rice dumplings into the river to distract the fish from his body while they searched for him.

Today people eat rice dumplings and race boats shaped like dragons to honor Qu Yuan's memory. Dragon boats are long and slim, sometimes over eighty-nine feet (27 m) long. The **prow** is carved in the shape of a huge dragon head and the **hull** is beautifully painted. Up to seventy rowers are needed to power each boat. The spectators cheer for their favorite teams, clang cymbals and gongs, and wave colorful flags. The dragon boat race is a noisy and exciting festival!

The rowers speed towards the finish line to the beat of the drum. The sternsman shouts "Row! Row! Row!" The crowd cheers the Dragon Boat racers on to success with cymbals, gongs, and colorful flags.

Although the Chinese practice modern western medicine, they also depend on traditional Chinese methods. These ancient healing techniques are 6,000 years old. Patients are treated with massage, medicinal herbs, acupuncture, exercise, and cupping.

Restoring the balance

Many Chinese people believe that illness is caused by an interruption in the *chi*, which is the vital energy of the body. Just as the *yin* and *yang* create a balance in the universe, these forces must also be balanced in the body so that the *chi* can flow properly. When the body is out of balance, a person becomes ill. A person with too much heat in his or her body, for example, might suffer from boils. Since heat is caused by the *yang*, the doctor will prescribe a *yin* remedy such as dandelions, which have a cooling effect to restore the balance of *yin* and *yang*.

(below) Many people practice tai chi *exercises to balance the energy in their bodies.*

Herbs and "dragon bones"

Treatment with medicinal herbs is the most popular kind of traditional Chinese medicine. A well-stocked herbalist carries up to 6,000 remedies. Wood, bark, and ten types of ginseng root are used as herbal-tea ingredients. Ground up animal parts, such as seashells and fossilized bones and teeth, known as "dragon bones," are also used as remedies.

Cures that kill animals

Each year, thousands of animals are killed to meet the demand for Chinese medical supplies. Some herbalists sell bear paws, rhinoceros horns, deer antlers, and sea horses. Some of these animals are **endangered species**. Hunters sometimes even kill pandas by accident while trying to trap other animals. There are only a thousand pandas left in the world! Poachers also hunt rhinoceroses, deer, tigers, and bears in other parts of the world such as Africa, India, and Canada. This practice angers many people.

The mystery of acupuncture

Acupuncture is an ancient way of treating illness by stimulating certain pressure points on the body. Thin, sterilized needles are painlessly inserted at key points on the body. Stimulating these points is said to balance the patient's *chi*.

Acupuncture is used to cure ailments, relieve pain, and anesthetize patients for surgery. An anesthetic is a substance that causes a patient to lose feeling in a certain area of his or her body. When acupuncture is used as an anesthetic, patients remain awake throughout an operation and can even talk to the doctor. Since they do not have to recover from any side effects due to a chemical anesthetic, patients can often leave the operating room by themselves!

Cupping

Cupping is another traditional technique used by Chinese doctors. Bamboo cups are immersed in hot water and are then applied to the body at acupuncture points. When the cup is put on the skin, the hot air inside cools and creates suction. The skin swells up into the cup as the blood beneath the surface rushes into the small surface vessels. Cupping is believed to relieve the congestion caused by asthma, the aches and pains that accompany **rheumatism**, and **bronchitis**.

Barefoot doctors

Barefoot doctors are not doctors without shoes. They are rural **paramedics** who are qualified to treat minor medical problems. They also educate people about health and personal hygiene. Barefoot doctors were once part-time rice farmers who worked in the fields in their bare feet, just like the other farmers. Now they are trained in both western and traditional medical techniques and work full time in clinics and country hospitals.

(right) Dentists advertise their skills with illustrated signs in a Kashgar bazaar. Kashgar is located in North Western China near the border with Pakistan.

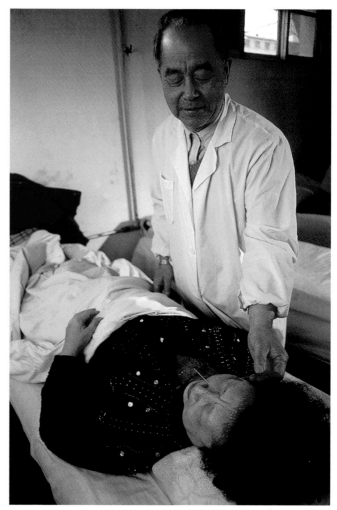

(above) A doctor inserts tiny needles into a patient's body as part of an acupuncture treatment.

The Chinese are passionate about their hobbies. Clusters of friends gather in the streets and parks to discuss their favorite pastimes. They might be stamp collectors, comparing and trading their treasures, or pet owners admiring one another's animals. Many people can also be seen playing a variety of traditional games.

Mah jong

Mah jong is a popular adult game. People play it with great enthusiasm. *Mah jong* is similar to the card game Gin Rummy, but it has a set of 136 tiles rather than fifty-two cards. Instead of hearts, diamonds, spades, and clubs, *mah jong* tiles are decorated with bamboo, circles, and characters. The sound of *mah jong* being played is as distinctive as the game itself. The loud clicking of tiles being moved furiously around the table top is a familiar noise to every *mah jong* player.

Chinese chess and checkers

Chinese chess is not the same as international chess. Like international chess, Chinese chess is played on a board and involves "taking" the opponent's pieces, but there are no knights, kings, or queens. Chinese chess is an ancient game that uses flat, round, black and white stones on a grid-patterned board. The Chinese watch large national chess tournaments with keen interest. They also have their own version of checkers played on a star-shaped board.

Children's games

Do you like playing hopscotch, marbles, ping pong or Cat's Cradle? Many children in China do as well! They meet after school to play all sorts of games. One game, called Five Stones, is similar to Jacks. Children also like to skip rope and draw pictures on the cement with chalk.

(top) These girls show off their shadow puppets. Maybe they will put on a shadow puppet show.

(left) Chinese checkers is played all over the world.

Fancy footwork

Another popular children's game is Kick-the-Bag. To play this game, a little bag is sewn together and filled with sand or grain. Then it is thrown into the air and kicked in the air over and over again with the inside of the heel. Kick-the-Bag can be played by one person or with others in a small circle. Another version of this game is called *ti jian zi*. Children find something light, such as a cork or a coin with a hole, and attach a feather to it for balance. They try to keep it in the air following rules similar to those of Kick-the-Bag. This game is far more difficult than it looks!

"Small games"

One of the best-loved hobbies in China is called "small games," or keeping pets. You may have a cat or a dog, but in China few families would have such a big animal for a pet. Cats and dogs are expensive to feed. Instead, Chinese people keep pigeons, singing birds, goldfish, and even crickets!

A pet or a pest?

In China, crickets have been kept as pets for thousands of years. Women at the imperial palace used to keep these singing insects in golden cages. Now, instead of golden cages, people use little bamboo baskets for their crickets. In winter, the owner puts a tiny hot-water bottle inside the basket to keep the cricket warm. Not only are crickets easy to feed, they are also easy to carry along in a pocket.

Champion crickets

Some owners take their crickets to fighting matches that attract large audiences. Everybody watches as the crickets are placed in a wooden bowl. A bowl is used as the fighting ring because the crickets cannot cling to the sides. To begin the match, the crickets are tickled with a hair on the end of a tiny stick. Everyone gets excited and cheers for his or her favorite dueling cricket.

(above) A young girl plays a game of ti jian zi on the street outside of her Beijing home.

Feathered friends

Many Chinese keep birds as pets. Elderly people often bring their songbirds to the park and hang their cages in the trees so their pets can be near other birds. It is delightful to hear all the birds sing together.

Some people keep pigeons. Owners attach homemade whistles to their pigeons' tails. As the birds fly through the air, the wind causes the whistles to blow. People with many pigeons give each one a different-sounding whistle. When the whole flock takes flight, it sounds like a symphony of flying whistles!

(above) Caring for caged songbirds is a favorite hobby of many elderly Chinese people.

☯ Try these activities ☯

Papercutting

The ancient tradition of papercutting is still used to decorate Chinese homes today. This folk art involves cutting complicated shapes out of colored paper. You can make your own Chinese papercut by using materials in your home. Glue, scissors, and several sheets of brightly colored paper are the supplies that you will need. Draw a simple design, such as a snowflake, on the back of a colored sheet of paper. Carefully snip out the shapes, and then turn the paper over. Paste the papercut down on a white piece of paper, let it dry, and then hang it up. Now try more complicated designs, such as that shown at the top of this page or the bottom of the opposite page. If you use red paper, the Chinese would say that good luck will soon come your way!

Wood and potato cuts

The traditional Chinese woodcut was used to capture images of beauty and peace. Woodcuts are made by engraving a design on one side of a wooden block. The carved side is coated with ink and pressed onto paper. The imprint of the design can be repeated over and over again by coating the woodcut with fresh ink each time.

Carving wood can be difficult. It requires special skill and the use of sharp woodworking tools. You can achieve a woodcut effect by carving a potato with a peeler or plastic knife. Cut a potato in half and carve a design into the surface. Remember to cut away all the flat area around your design. When you have finished your cutting, fill the bottom of a pie plate with watercolor paint. Dip the potato into the paint and make a print on a piece of paper. Make other potato-print designs and combine them to create more complicated patterns.

Eating with chopsticks

Instead of using a knife and fork for eating, Chinese people use chopsticks. Can you use these utensils? One chopstick is held between the thumb and the ring finger, and it never moves. The other chopstick is held by the tip of the thumb and the index and middle fingers. Remember to keep the tips even. It may seem difficult the first time you try but, with practice, it will become easy. In China even the smallest children use chopsticks!

Your own Chinese opera

Create a Chinese opera in your classroom or with your neighborhood friends. Decide on a story based on a historical, school, or neighborhood event. Write an outline of the story and decide which parts you and your friends will play.

Chinese operas include singing, dancing, acrobatics, and pantomime. The actors learn both their lines and gestures. Colors are important, too. Red stands for loyalty, black for boldness, and white for evil.

Costumes, makeup, gestures

Devise a set of costume and makeup clues. Remember that in a real Chinese opera, costumes help identify the characters and makeup tells whether a character is good or evil, brave or fearful. Movements of the sleeves, arms and hands can give the setting for your story. For example, outstretched arms show that it is dark. You can invent five or ten different settings, such as: bent left elbow to show morning, or outstretched fingers to indicate school time. Be sure to share these clues with your audience so they can participate in your story. Perhaps you can get them to shout out words such as "school time," or "nighttime," when a setting has changed.

Your performance

Once you have a basic outline for your performance, you can let the characters fill in their own dialogue in the script and create their own gestures. Make sure all the players learn their parts. Use dramatic and exaggerated actions. Prance, pitter patter, and pirouette. Let everyone have a turn bellowing and squealing, hitting high and low notes.

You can stay in the opera mood at home by telling your parents about your school day in song instead of speech. Get your whole family to participate at dinner. They can sing, "Pass the peas, please!" with great flourish.

In Chinese opera sleeve movements and arm positions have specific meanings. What might this gesture mean?

Improvise and have fun!

After having put on a structured Chinese-style opera, you may want to give another performance using your own style of opera. This time, do not learn lines. Improvise instead. Make your own set of rules and get dramatic!

Glossary

ancestors People from whom one is descended

bronchitis An illness caused by an infection of the tiny tubes in the lungs

Buddha An ancient religious leader from India

Buddhism A religion founded by Buddha

calligraphy The art of fine handwriting

communist - Describing an economic system in which the country's resources are held in common by all the people and regulated by the government

Confucius An ancient Chinese scholar whose ideas have greatly influenced Chinese society

culture The customs, beliefs, and arts of a distinct group of people. Culture also means the result of an interest in literature, history, and fine arts.

endangered species A species of animal that is very close to becoming extinct

Forbidden City A public museum in Beijing. It was originally a palace built in the 15th century, which only government officials and members of the emperor's family could enter.

hemp A strong plant fiber used to make rope

hull The bottom and sides of a ship

incense A substance that produces a sweet-smelling smoke when burned

lodestone A type of iron ore that is naturally magnetized and can be used to indicate direction

lunar Relating to the moon

Mao Zedong Founder of the Chinese Communist Party and China's leader for twenty-seven years

Miao One of China's fifty-six national groups who live in Guizhou province

missionaries People sent by a church to spread their religion to those who do not yet believe in it

Mongol One of China's fifty-six national groups, who live in the autonomous region of Inner Mongolia

myth A legend or story that tries to explain mysterious events or ideas

national group People who share a common background and lifestyle

paramedic A trained medical worker capable of performing basic medical procedures

percussion Relating to musical instruments that require striking

pictograph A picture used to represent a word

porcelain A type of fine pottery

prophet A religious leader believed to be inspired by God or a spirit

prow The front part of a boat

relic Something or a piece of something that has survived from the past

rheumatism A painful condition that causes swollen and stiff muscles, bones, joints, and nerves

rural Relating to the countryside

sculpture The art of making figures by carving materials such as rock, wood, or ice

symbol Something that represents or stands for something else

Taoism A religion based on the teachings of Laotzu, an ancient Chinese philosopher

Tibetan One of China's fifty-six national groups, who live in the autonomous region of Tibet

tradition A long-held custom or practice

western The term used to describe people from the western part of the world, especially Europe and North America, as opposed to people from Asia, such as the Chinese and Japanese

Index

2 3 4 5 6 7 8 9 0 Printed in the USA 5 4 3 2 1